AFRICAN ANIMALS
THROUGH
AFRICAN EYES

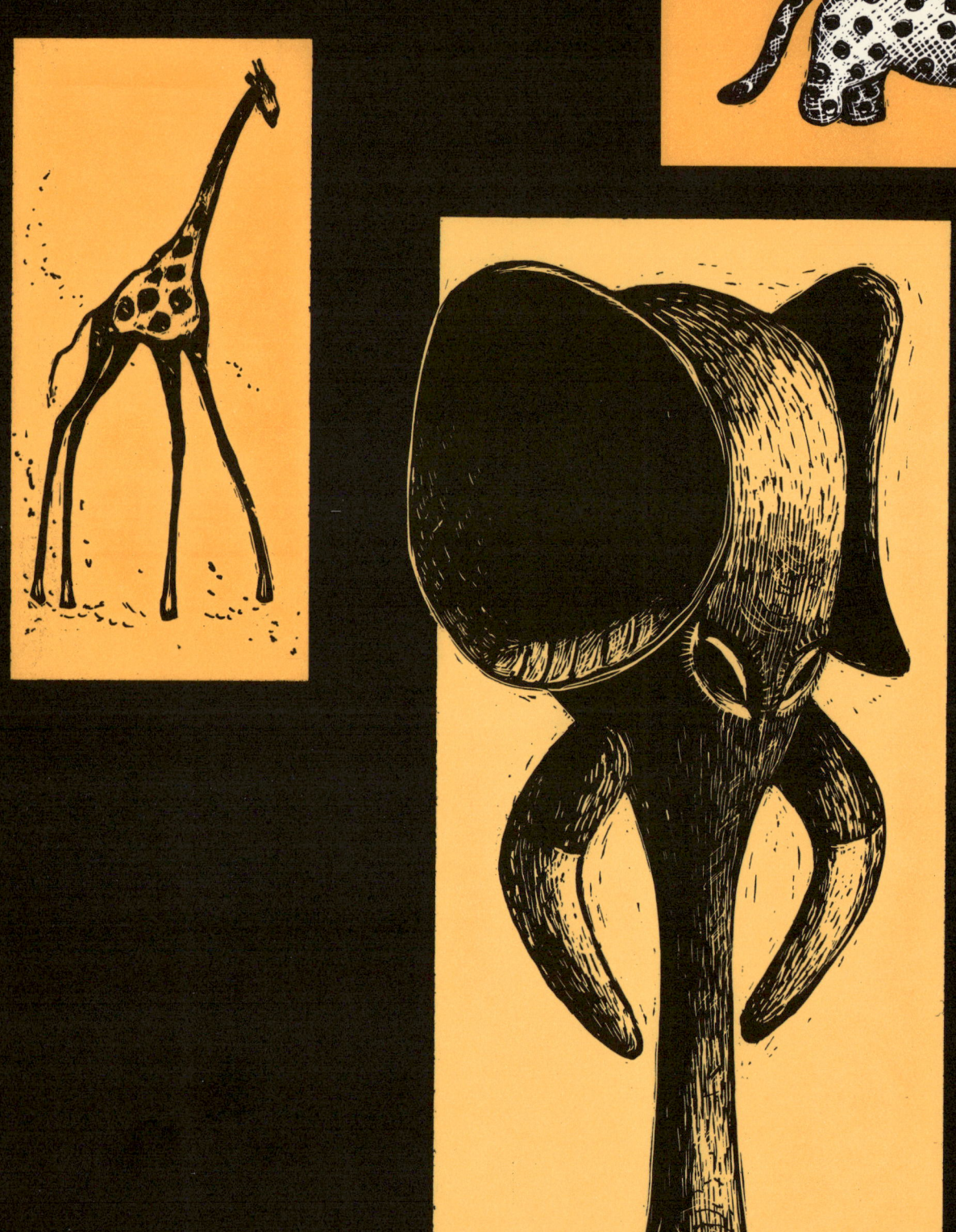

AFRICAN ANIMALS THROUGH AFRICAN EYES

JANET and ALEX D'AMATO

 Julian Messner • New York

A Note to the Reader

We are grateful to the Museum of Primitive Art in New York City for their help in providing material for this book. Whenever possible, ancient or early examples of African art were selected to illustrate the animals described, or pieces were chosen that represented purely tribal art. Only beliefs and art that were true to a particular tribe and region were included. The areas north of the Sahara, Egypt and Ethopia are not included.

The illustrations in this book were redrawn from exhibits and photographs of objects in museums and private collections. In order to give a more vivid picture, some are composites. The scenes in the cave paintings are from several different caves at one general location. In cases where only fragments were found, the drawings show them, wherever possible, restored into completed shapes.

Published by Julian Messner, a division of Simon & Schuster, Inc., 1 West 39 Street, New York, N.Y. 10018. All rights reserved.
Copyright © 1971 by Janet and Alex D'Amato
Printed in the United States of America
ISBN 0-671-32425-X Cloth Trade
    0-671-32426-8 MCE
Library of Congress Catalog Card No. 70-154970

contents

FOREWORD 9

THE SAHARA DESERT 13
    An ancient well populated grassland
        The camel

THE WESTERN GRASSLANDS 15
    Of kingdoms, cattle and an animal trickster
        The antelope, the buffalo, cattle,
        the horse, the hare

THE WESTERN FORESTS 22
    Royal leopards, bronze sculptures, and sacrifices
        The leopard, the fire-spitter, the goat and
        the chicken, the spider, the ram

THE EASTERN GRASSLANDS 34
    Of ivory and a lost past
        The elephant, the rhinoceros,
        the giraffe, the lion

THE JUNGLE 39
    Realm of the Congo
        The monkey, the dog

REPTILES AND FISH 43
    Of sea gods and totems
        The crocodile, the mudfish, the chameleon,
        the lizard, the snake

WILD BIRDS 51
    And other winged things
        The hornbill, the eagle and hawk,
        the bat, the butterfly

CONCLUSION 60

MAPS 62-63

Books by JANET and ALEX D'AMATO

AFRICAN ANIMALS THROUGH AFRICAN EYES

AFRICAN CRAFTS FOR YOU TO MAKE

INDIAN CRAFTS

CARDBOARD CARPENTRY

HANDICRAFTS FOR HOLIDAYS

▶

Opposite page: Outlines of animals carved in rock walls at Tassili

foreword

Since the earliest times, people and animals have shared the continent of Africa. Much of the history of Africa before the arrival of the first Europeans is now lost to us. Little is known because nothing was *written* that described those times or the life of the people who lived there.

But there are clues to tell us how men lived long ago and how they felt about the animals around them. Some of these clues can be found in bones of animals and pieces of ancient carvings that archeologists have dug up from sand and soil. Other clues are in cave paintings done long ago which show scenes of farming, cattle-raising, fishing, and hunting.

Still another way we learn of African beliefs is through myths, legends, and folktales. We are very fortunate that some stories from the past have survived to tell us about African customs, culture, and religion.

The animals of Africa play a big part in tribal religious beliefs. Most tribal religions agree that there is a supreme god, who made the world and everything in it. But they also believe the affairs of the world were left to lesser gods, or were taken over by evil spirits. The weather, the seasons, the crops, and the lives of the people were all controlled by these lesser gods. The name and character of each god varied greatly from tribe to tribe. Some tribes believed these gods appeared on earth in animal form.

There was also the belief that when someone died, his spirit took another form. Often, a dead ancestor was believed to dwell in an animal or in a carved figure. But no matter what form they appeared in, the people believed that the gods and spirits lived very close to them and took a large part in their affairs. Rituals, ceremonies, and magic were used by the people to please or influence these spirits and were part of almost every act in their daily life.

Like stories and religious beliefs, carvings give some clues to the past. The methods and styles used in making a carved figure were handed down from father to son. Thus, for many generations, animal carvings were done much the same way, not to make a work of art but usually for a religious purpose. Sometimes carvings were made for adornment of a king's court. Wood carvings, as well as sculptures in metal, clay, and stone were not meant to be exact copies of the animals they represented. Instead, they often represented a god or spirit who was believed to have taken the form of an animal. Their art was a link from the people to their gods or ancestors.

▶

Cave paintings from the Saraha showed a man in a reed boat hunting a hippopotamus, while other hunters stalked antelopes or rabbits.

Of course, Africans also used animals in many practical ways. Animals provided a major source of food, and hides and furs were made into clothing and household items. Horn and bone were sometimes used in musical instruments or carved tools and ornaments. Even the teeth and claws of animals were put to use, for the people made decorations and jewelry from them.

The various tribes thought of the same animal in different ways. To one tribe, a particular animal was merely a source of food. But another tribe might believe this same animal represented a god or ancestor, and so members of that tribe were not allowed to harm it.

From their myths and fables, carvings and paintings of animals, we have some idea of what the plentiful animals and other creatures meant to these African peoples of the past.

The Sahara Desert

An ancient well-populated grassland

Very long ago, when men were just beginning to live together in groups, the large parts of North Africa that are now desert were covered by grassy plains. Vast herds of wild animals lived in the Sahara, the area west of the Nile River. The people farmed, raised cattle, and fished in the rivers. We know this because archeologists have found the bones of these people and animals in the sands of the desert.

Clues to what life was like in the ancient Sahara have been found in the form of paintings made by men on the rock walls of caves. These paintings portray lively scenes of hunting, cattle-herding, and family life. In these scenes are many pictures of animals. Giraffes, rhinoceros, fish, and many kinds of gazelles appear in life-like detail. Scientists believe the paintings were done as long ago as 5000 B.C.

However, the people who made the Sahara cave paintings were not able to continue living on the land. By 2000 B.C., their crops had become poor, and the rivers had begun to dry up. No one knows why. Perhaps, worldwide changes in climate had cut down the rainfall in the area. Perhaps, the cattle had grazed the grass too short and left the ground bare. In any case, by 1500 B.C., the Sahara was already becoming the desert it is today. The people and animals moved south to land that was less dry. But they left behind the cave paintings that tell us how important animals were in the Africa of this ancient period.

◀

These scenes from several caves at Tassili in the Saraha showed early cattle raising. The experts who studied the paintings found that people of many different races were included.

THE CAMEL For centuries, the hot, dry Sahara made travel between East and West Africa difficult. Then, about 600 B.C., the camel was brought to Africa by traders from the Middle East, the lands at the eastern end of the Mediterranean Sea. This beast, the one-humped dromedary or camel, was able to live in the desert whereas horses or cattle could not. These camels were very tough, and they could travel tirelessly with little food or water for many days. They could also carry heavy loads.

The arrival of the camels made it possible to cross the Sahara once again. Soon, caravan routes opened up communication between West Africa and the lands to the east. West African gold and ivory were traded for salt and other products from Egypt and other areas.

Centuries later, the great empire of Mali occupied a large part of the western grassland. Like the previous local kingdoms, Mali depended largely on the camel for trade and for transportation. In 1352 A.D., Mali's most famous king, Mansa Musa, made a religious pilgrimage across the Sahara to the holy city of Mecca in Arabia. He rode at the head of a camel caravan, which carried sixty thousand people and one hundred camel-loads of pure gold!

This creature shaped in a special hardened clay called terra cotta was found in the northern Niger River area. It was probably meant to be a camel.

The Western Grasslands

Of kingdoms, cattle, and an animal trickster

Between the western Sahara and the forests along the coast of the Gulf of Guinea lies a wide area of grassland. Most of these areas are now parts of the nations of Mali and Niger, but the grasslands were once much larger.

In ancient times, the plentiful animals of the grasslands were hunted by men who used weapons of wood or stone. When the people of this area learned to make iron (no one knows exactly when or how), their lives changed considerably. Sharper weapons and stronger tools made it easier both to hunt animals and to farm. The people had more time to develop skills and to trade, and they began to live together in towns. By 300 A.D., some of the towns had grown into powerful kingdoms. The people of these kingdoms used iron weapons to conquer other peoples.

The rulers of these kingdoms had courts of great splendor. Iron had not only brought increased trade and conquest, but also better ways of carving. The royal courts were often decorated with statues of men and animals that had been carved with iron tools. Sometimes, the statues themselves were made of iron.

The common people of the time lived in grass-roofed houses in villages. They were mainly farmers, fishermen, and skilled tradesmen. The iron-workers, wood-carvers, and other craftsmen of these villages made statues and masks which were often shaped like animals. Usually, these objects were used for religious purposes. They are the only things which have survived to tell us about the life of the kingdoms of the grasslands.

Statues and masks were made according to traditions which were handed down from parent to child for many generations. The people believed that the tree whose wood was going to be carved was a living thing, like an animal or a human being. Therefore, they felt that the tree had to give them permission to cut it down and carve it. To these Africans, animals, plants, and men were joined together in a world of regularly changing times and seasons. Throughout the year, they celebrated natural events such as springtime, harvest, and birth in special ceremonies.

THE ANTELOPE A myth of the Bambara tribe of Mali tells of Chi Wara, the god of growth. One day, Chi Wara came to earth in the form of an antelope, a very common animal in the grasslands. As an antelope, this god showed men how to grow their food, rather than having to hunt for it. Thereafter, a dance was held each spring in honor of Chi Wara, in the hope that he would grant his people a good growing season. The leader of the dance wore on his head a carved figure of the god in antelope form. Chi Wara was also honored by a dance during the fall harvest season. During both these ceremonies, the dancers leaped high in the air, imitating the graceful bounds of the antelope.

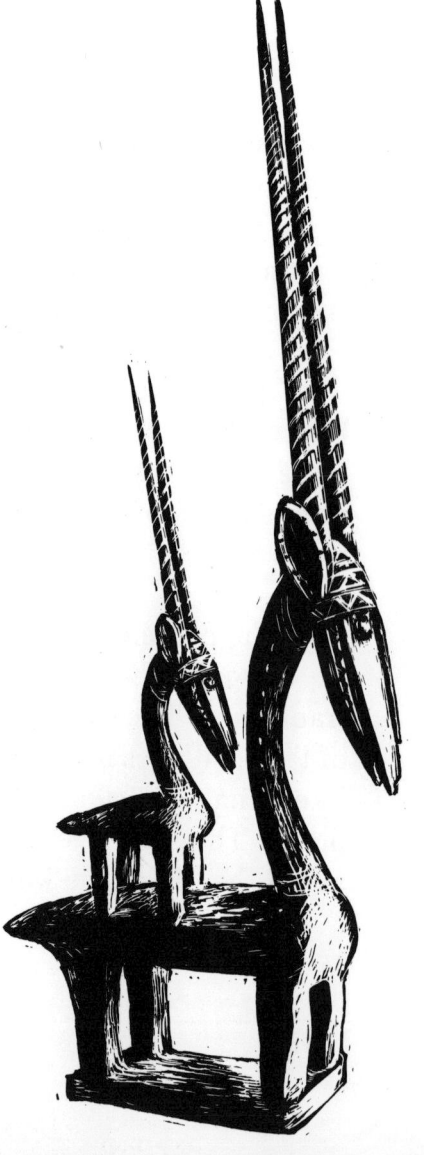

The Chi Wara headdress had many shapes, some representing the male antelope with an ornamental mane. Others, like the one shown, represented the female with a young one on her back.

To the Kurumba people of the Upper Volta, this fanciful carving represented a different spirit from the Bambara's antelope. They wore this headdress in ceremonies after a funeral to please the ancestor spirits, hoping the spirits would go back to where they should be.

THE BUFFALO Another hoofed animal which lived in the grasslands was the evil-tempered African buffalo. This beast was both feared and respected by the people. In Buganda, when a man killed a buffalo, he built a small hut and put the head of the dead animal inside. In that way, he hoped to satisfy the angry spirit of the buffalo so it would not follow him back to his village.

Hardly any examples of carvings of cattle can be found because the people who loved cattle were wanderers, who traveled with their herds. Therefore, they made no permanent sculptures. This example from the coast of Guinea was a ceremonial leather head covering with real oxen horns, red seed and shell decorations.

CATTLE

The herding of cattle is a very old occupation in western Africa. Even today, some tribes, such as the Fulani, count a man's wealth by the number of cattle he owns. The Fulani have no permanent homes, and they constantly follow their cattle to new grazing lands. The Fulani raise cattle for milk rather than meat, and their entire way of life is centered around their herds. One of their legends tells about the first herdsmen.

Way back at the beginning of time, a young boy was walking by a river when he heard the water god call out to him: "Do you want to help your people?" The boy nodded.

"Then you must walk away from the river and never look back," said the water god.

So the boy began walking in the direction he had been told. He heard strange noises behind him, but he knew he must not look back. He walked on and on. The sounds grew even louder and the earth began to shake. Finally, the boy could not resist looking back. He saw a herd of strange beasts coming out of the river and following him. As soon as he turned to look at them, the cattle stopped coming out of the river. But a vast herd had already gathered, so the boy took them home to his people. Ever since, the men of that tribe have been cattle herders.

The Fulani have a proverb: He who harms cattle harms the Fulani.

A ceremonial dance of the Upper Volta region featured the buffalo, a tribal animal. Other masked figures represented the hornbill and the antelope.

THE HORSE

Cave pictures indicate that the horse has been in Africa since at least 1200 B.C. The early kingdoms of the grasslands depended on horses to carry their warriors into battle. In 1067 A.D., one of these armies had two hundred thousand mounted warriors!

The ancient West African kingdoms were well known for their mounted troops, whose horse-trappings were often covered with gold. One clan did nothing but care for the horses and their luxurious stables.

Since it was horses which carried the warriors to victory, it is easy to see why horses were valued so highly in these lands. Statues of men on horseback were usually the figures of kings or important leaders. Sometimes the mounted figure was that of a spirit, sometimes even a god.

THE HARE

Smaller animals also appear in the tales and carvings of the grasslands. A favorite type of African fable is one in which a weak creature, such as the hare, overcomes a larger and stronger one by cunning. These stories express the feelings of every human being who has ever felt himself helpless when faced with problems he cannot solve.

There are countless tales about a hare's pranks and the mischief he gets himself into. A lazy beast, the hare often talks other animals into doing his work for him. Sometimes, he steals things and then easily convinces the owners that someone else is guilty. The hare is a practical joker too. He may muddy up a water hole (a serious thing in a dry country) and then see that another animal, such as a lizard or a baboon, is punished for it.

The hare's role is not always the same in these tales. Sometimes, he is the only animal that is able to overcome a beast as fearsome as the lion—always by using sly tricks. At other times, his tricks are cruel, and he may be punished in the end. Yet he is always a weakling who uses his wits instead of his strength.

Horse with rider and attendant. This metal statue was found in the Niger River region.

The Western Forests

Royal leopards, bronze sculptures, and sacrifices

In the bulge of western Africa are forests, which vary in kind from dense woodland to steamy rain forest. The people of these western forests produced some of the finest animal sculpture of Africa. Their skill in working with wood, metal, and clay has given us unforgettable pictures of the life and customs of times past.

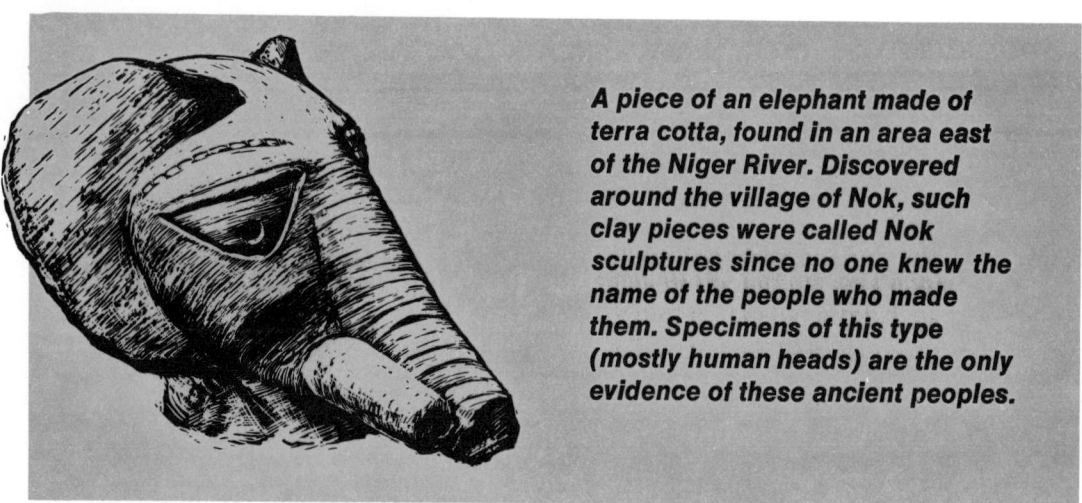

A piece of an elephant made of terra cotta, found in an area east of the Niger River. Discovered around the village of Nok, such clay pieces were called Nok sculptures since no one knew the name of the people who made them. Specimens of this type (mostly human heads) are the only evidence of these ancient peoples.

The earliest animal figures that have come down to us from the western forest were made as long ago as 1000 B.C. by the people who lived along the Niger River. Later, in the same area, the kingdom of Ife arose, which brought the art of bronze sculpture to new heights. It is known that in about 1300 A.D., a messenger came to Ife from the kingdom of Benin (further south), asking for a craftsman to teach the workers of Benin how to cast bronze.

A bell made by the craftsmen of Benin which was probably used in ceremonies or as an altar decoration. Cast in bronze were a delicately shaped head of the king and twelve mudfish, his royal creatures.

This casting was a complicated process. First, the figure had to be shaped in wax. Then it was covered with clay. When the clay hardened, the wax was melted out, leaving a mold. Next, molten bronze was poured into the mold. When the metal had cooled, the clay was broken away. The final step was to file and finish the bronze. This method is known as the lost wax process, and it is used today by sculptors throughout the world.

The craftsman from Ife who taught the lost wax process to the people of Benin was named Igueghae. In gratitude, Benin's guild of bronze-makers made him a national hero. They later produced beautiful bronzes which were alive with birds, animals, and fish, as well as kings and warriors.

These decorative bronze panels help to visualize what the court of the Oba (king) of Benin must have been like. The wooden posts of the courtyard and palace were covered with these panels. They showed soliders, hunters, leopards and other animals. Birds, fish, the costumes of the people were all shown in great detail. The king, as he sat on his throne (an elaborately carved stool), was surrounded by elegantly dressed attendants and royal leopards. He wore ornaments and jewelry of gold, intricately carved ivory and strands of coral beads. The room was probably decorated with many statues, carvings and huge ivory tusks carved in great detail. Bronze bells, drums, gongs and other instruments added to every ceremony. All art was made to show the power and wealth of the king.

Along the Volta River were gold mines so rich that the region became known as the Gold Coast. Among the people called the Ashanti, the form of money used was gold dust. This fact led to the development of an interesting art form. The custom was to weigh out quantities of gold dust using bronze weights. The earliest weights were merely lumps of bronze of the right size. Later, however, the weights were made so as to be decorative. They were cast into all sorts of fanciful shapes by the use of the lost wax method. Many were no more than two inches high, but they had the form of animals, plants, or people. Some of the weights illustrated scenes from fables.

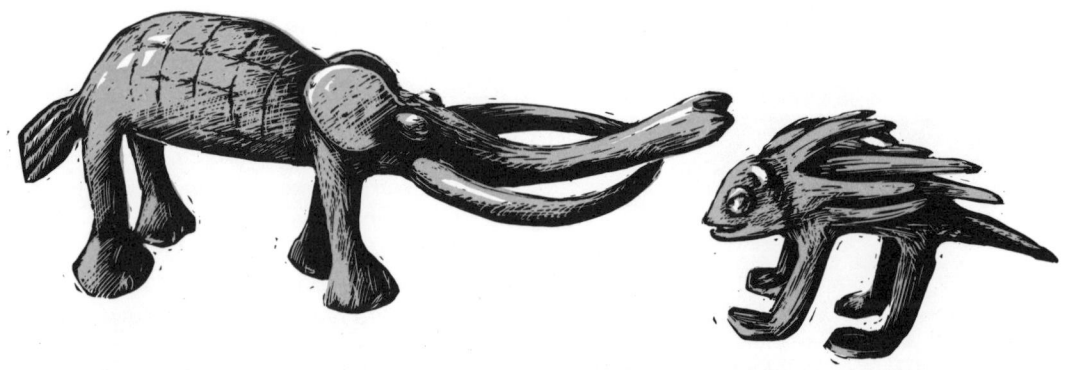

Three examples of Ashanti gold weights: an elephant, a porcupine and a monkey eating fruit from a tree.

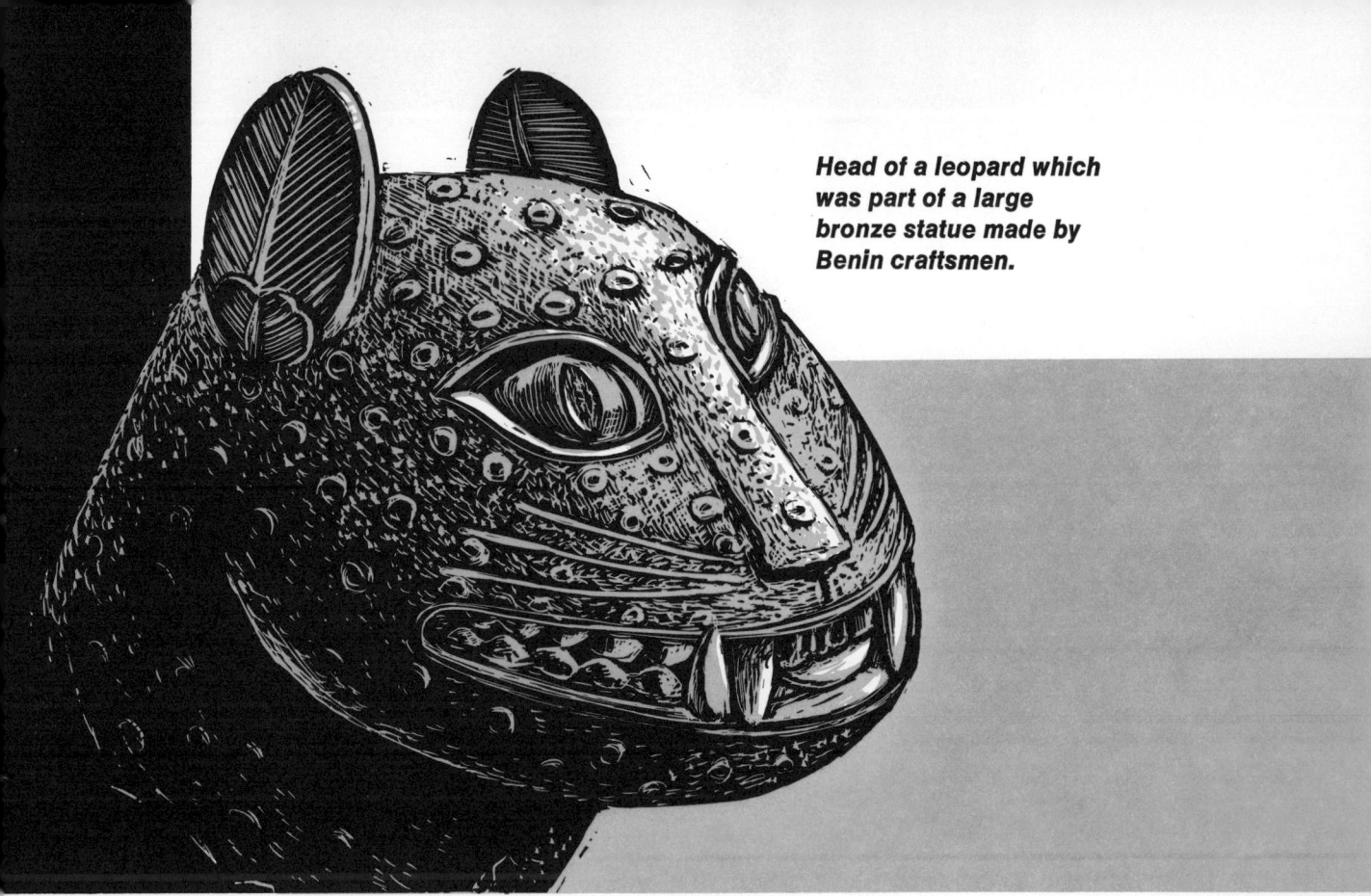

Head of a leopard which was part of a large bronze statue made by Benin craftsmen.

THE LEOPARD

A very fierce and beautiful animal once common in the forests of western Africa was the leopard. In Benin, he was a symbol of royalty. Throughout the king's residence, there were statues of leopards in ivory, bronze, and wood. The ceremonial jars used for pouring water for the king were also in the shape of leopards, as were the gold or ivory ornaments and the jewelry worn by the members of the court.

In other parts of Africa, such as Gaboon, and among the Fon tribes of Dahomey, the leopard was a sign of terror rather than of power. Secret groups called Leopard Societies committed acts of murder and cannibalism. A man was required to kill a member of his own family in order to join one of these societies. The members dressed in leopard skins and carried claw-shaped knives.

THE FIRE-SPITTER

The Senufo tribe of the Ivory Coast created a ceremonial mask which combined the features of several animals in order to be as terrifying as possible. This mask was called the fire-spitter. It had the powerful jaws of the crocodile, the tusks of the warthog, and the horns of the antelope. Often, other creatures such as birds, chameleons, and snakes were shown crawling on the mask. Some of the masks were two-sided, with jaws both front and back.

The fire-spitter was so fearful-looking that it was thought to be dangerous just to touch the costume worn with it. The mask was supposed to frighten away evil spirits or witches that were threatening the people. The men of the tribe kept the mask in a secret grove except when it was in use. Then, on a dark night, drums would beat and a horrifying figure would appear. Running and stomping, the fire-spitter would chase away evil spirits.

The most impressive part of the ceremony was that the figure really appeared to spit fire. Inside the mask's huge jaws was a clever arrangement of glowing coals and bits of grass coated with resin. When the person inside the mask blew on the coals, a stream of orange sparks shot out into the night. The people believed that this sight was sure to frighten away the demons, so no harm would come to the village.

The dancer performed the ceremony of the firespitter around a fire.

THE GOAT AND THE CHICKEN

Another way these people kept themselves safe from evil spirits was by making a sacrifice. For that purpose, the animals most often used were the goat and the chicken. Both have been domesticated in Africa since ancient times. Therefore, they were available when needed. The purpose of the sacrifice was to win the favor of the gods by giving them something of value. If the gods were pleased, they would not send such disasters as floods, famines, and disease. A goat was the usual sacrifice, but a chicken might be used for less important problems.

In addition to being used for sacrifices, chickens sometimes served to tell whether a man was guilty or innocent of a crime. The medicine man, who acted as judge, first questioned the suspect. Then he gave a dose of poison to a chicken. If the chicken died, it was considered a sign from the gods that the man was guilty. This method was thought to be more fair than if the people had just asked the opinion of the medicine man, who might have personal reasons for his answer. However, the medicine man could have varied the dosage of the poison in such a way that the chicken would die only if he believed that the suspect was guilty.

In one story from Nigeria, the chicken plays a role in the creation of the world. The creator god, Olorun, had made the world and the many lesser gods who lived in heaven. But down

An Ashanti bronze goat used for weighing gold.

Ashanti bronze weight of a medicine man preparing to sacrifice a chicken.

below, there was nothing but watery marshes. Olorun sent a god named Obatala down to make some dry land. Obatala dumped a huge snailshell full of dirt into the water, and on the mound of dirt he set sixteen sacred chickens. For four days, the chickens scratched about, and they made the dry land on which was located the center of the world, the city of Ife. The fifth day was set aside for praising the creator, Olorun. Then, in the next four days, Olorun created the other birds, trees, people, and animals. And that is how the world was made.

The importance of the chicken in African life is shown by the fact that it was the subject of so many proverbs. For example: "A blind chicken scratches what others will eat." Also: "Rooster, don't make so much noise; your mother was only an egg."

Benin bronze rooster. It was probably placed on an altar for an ancestor, usually the king's mother. In smaller villages in the area, wooden cocks were made for the same purpose for the chief's mother.

THE SPIDER Many West African fables are about the spider. His web is said to stretch from earth to heaven, so he carries messages from gods to men.

In the stories of the Ashanti people, the spider hero, Anansi, is very clever. He is the one who brought the art of story-telling to the people from the gods. Like the hare in the stories from the grasslands, Anansi is a trickster. In spite of his small size, he often outwits men and other larger creatures.

THE RAM

Another animal of western Africa that was known for its power was the ram. The ram was most often associated with Shango, the thunder god. The sound of thunder was believed to be either the voice of the ram or the stamping of his feet. Shango was feared because he was a god of storms. But he was also considered helpful in that he brought rain.

Worshippers of Shango were sometimes portrayed with a double-headed axe. The axe represented lightning, which also splits trees. Among the Yoruba people of West Africa, there was a ceremony in which Shango was worshipped by pouring ram's blood over a carved figure with a double-headed axe.

The top of this statue of a priestess of the worshippers of Shango showed the double headed axe.

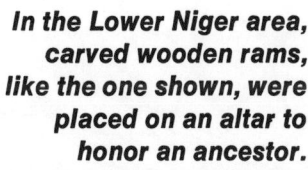

In the Lower Niger area, carved wooden rams, like the one shown, were placed on an altar to honor an ancestor.

the eastern grasslands

Of ivory and a lost past

In East Africa, as in West Africa, large areas covered by grasslands supported vast herds of animals. Antelopes, gazelles, zebras, rhinoceros, cheetahs, elephants, giraffes, lions, and hyenas have shared these great plains for centuries with many groups of people.

Parts of what are now Zambia and Rhodesia are the sites of cave paintings which were done as long ago as 5000 B.C. Animals are portrayed in many of the paintings, which were probably made as part of magical and religious ceremonies. Drawing an animal's picture was supposed to give a man power over that animal so he would be successful in hunting.

These Bushman cave paintings from Rhodesia showed zebras and other animals of the grasslands of long ago.

This tiny, pure gold rhinoceros was discovered in a grave site near the Limpopo River.

The cave paintings are not the only evidence of the importance of animals to the people of ancient East Africa. In the stone fortress of Zimbabwe, which lies between the Limpopo and Zambesi rivers, were found many stone sculptures of birds and animals. We know very little about the people of Zimbabwe, but it seems likely that they rose to power because they controlled the rich trade between the inland centers and the coastal towns as far back as 300 A.D. For several centuries, the coastal towns traded with countries as far away as India and China.

Possibly the rulers of these inland empires lived in fortresses like Zimbabwe. Their wealth came from metals mined in the interior and from animal products. Two animals in particular were important to East Africa's trade. One was the rhinoceros, whose horn was greatly valued by the Chinese for its supposedly magical powers. The other was the African elephant, which produced the world's finest ivory.

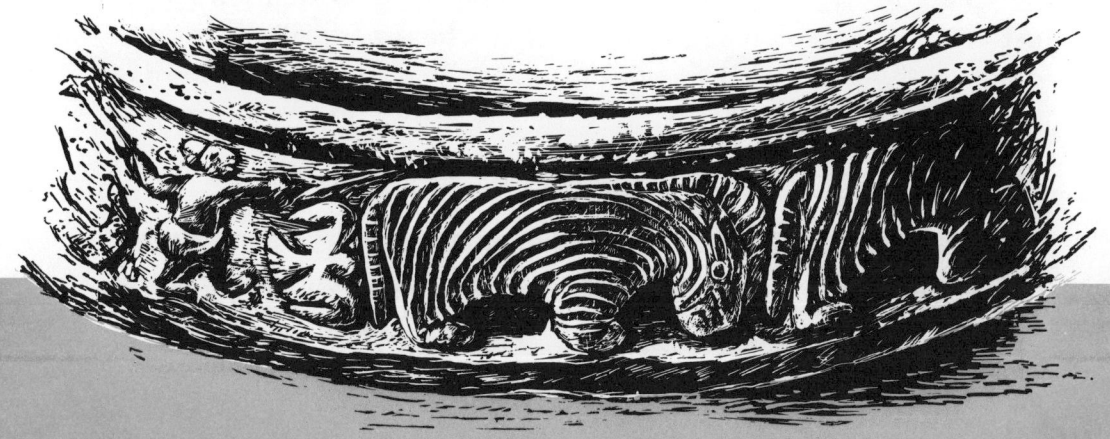

Carved on the side of a stone ceremonial bowl found near Zimbabwe, a bird and a man follow zebras around.

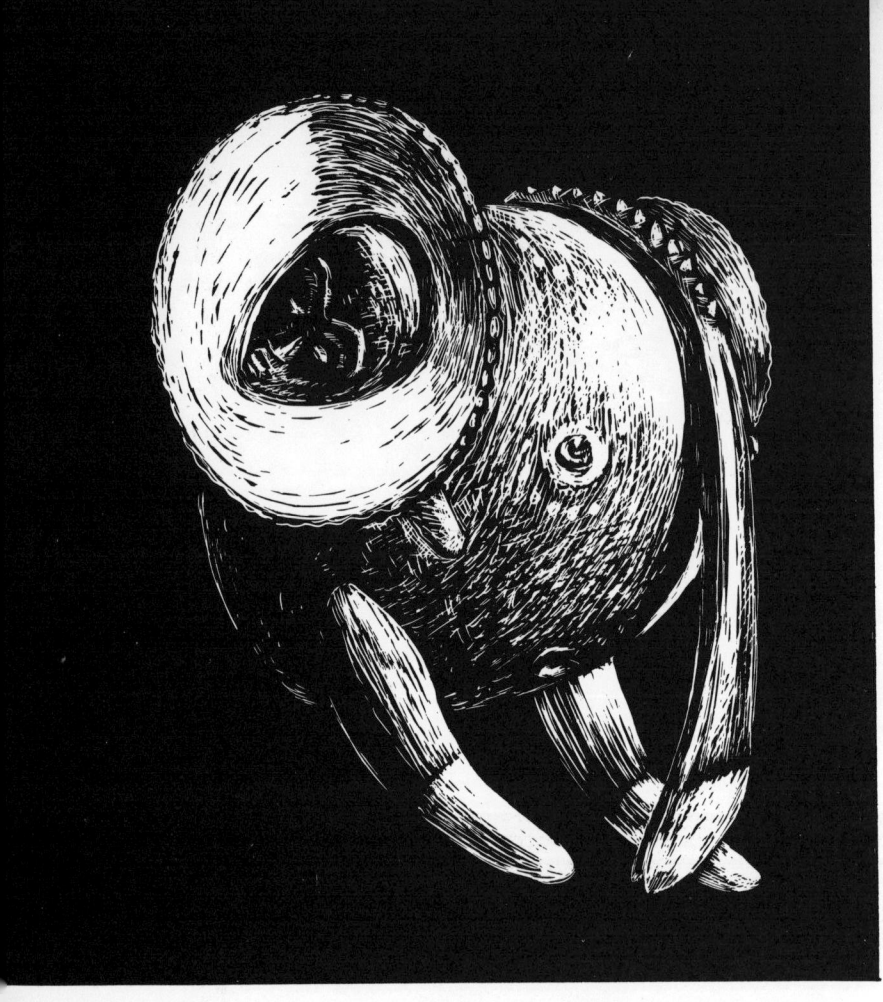

Although it is believed ancient craftsmen of East Africa made carvings, few have survived. Most have been broken, rotted away or buried. Later tribes were wanderers who made no sculptures. Therefore, this example of an elephant carved of wood was from West Africa, and was made by the Baule people of the Ivory Coast.

THE ELEPHANT From the most ancient times to the present, the elephant has been hunted for the ivory of his tusks. Although it was once found in most of Africa, the elephant is now rare in many parts of that continent because it has been hunted continuously. The fact that the ivory of the African elephant is whiter and less brittle than that of the Indian elephant has made it the prime target of the ivory trade. Hunting not only cut down the herds, it also brought wealth to many of the tribes living along the trade routes.

The carving of ivory is an ancient art. Ivory is beautiful and smooth, and it is easy to work with. African artists used it to make some of their finest ornaments and statuettes, which were often carried to distant lands as gifts for kings and emperors.

The rhinoceros was once common in the grasslands of Africa. Hunted for the value of its horn or just because of its rather ugly appearance, it has become quite rare. Long ago, Bushmen made this rhinoceros shape by chipping into a rock wall at the edge of the desert in Botswana.

THE GIRAFFE

Another creature which has been valued by the men of East Africa is the giraffe. Over the centuries, some hunted the giraffe for its meat, others sought its hide, which was used for clothing or household objects. In one place, the gentle and graceful giraffe had even been killed just for its tail, which was made into fly whisks.

THE LION

The grassy plains of Africa are also the home of the lion. No matter where it has been found, this magnificent member of the cat family has always been a symbol of royal power to men. In many parts of East Africa, rituals are performed and charms are worn in order to give men the strength and courage of the lion. In certain Zulu tribes, only the chief was once allowed to wear a lionskin robe and lion's mane decorations.

Yet in spite of the great awe in which the lion was held, African fables often tell how he is tricked and defeated by weaker animals. The people of Angola say that a hunter once found a lion caught in a trap. The lion begged to be set free and promised that in return he would help the man in his hunting and would never harm him. The man agreed, and he set the great beast loose. However, the lion soon got hungry, and he asked permission to eat the man's arm. Quite naturally, the man did not agree, and an argument followed.

The man and the lion asked a wise turtle to be judge of the matter. "I cannot decide until I see exactly what happened," the turtle declared. "You will have to show me from the beginning."

So the man and the lion took the turtle to where the trap was, and the lion went inside to show how things had been at the beginning. "Of course," said the wise turtle. "Now I see what happened." And he and the man went away together, leaving the lion trapped.

A bronze lion found in a grave in the upper Nile area. In some areas, the lion was believed to represent the sun because of his yellowish color and by the way his mane surrounded his face.

The Jungle

Realm of the Congo

The tropical jungle which covers the area of the Congo River basin was the home of many different tribes and animals. Most villages were small, and were built in clearings between the trees.

At times in the past, however, the region saw the rise and fall of great kingdoms which sometimes lasted for centuries. Since these kingdoms were for the most part cut off from the rest of Africa by the thickness of the jungle, the people there developed arts, crafts, and beliefs that were quite different from those of other areas. Of course, the animals of their stories and carvings are often different, too, because the creatures that live in the jungle are not always the same as those of the grassland and the forest.

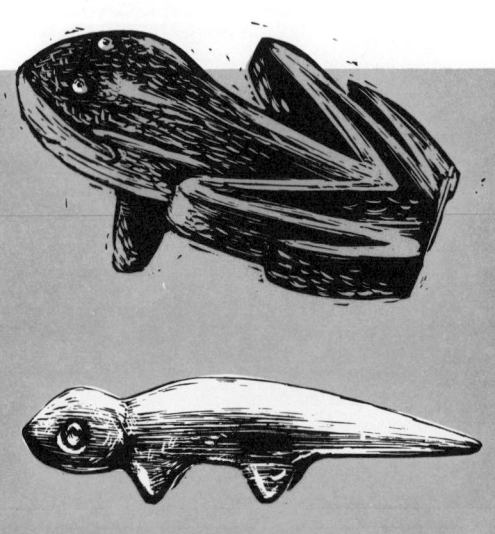

These three creatures are from various tribes of the Congo. The large wooden animal (left) was carved on top of a mask. The frog was carved of wood. The lizard like shape was carved of ivory and may have been an amulet.

This wooden mask from the Cameroons was worn at an angle on top of the head. It was believed to give protection or power to certain people who deserved it.

THE MONKEY The Congo jungles are the home of many kinds of monkeys. They are the clowns of the area. Even in serious religious ceremonies, the dancers masked like monkeys were generally for entertainment only.

From the coastal region of the Congo comes the story of a monkey who was almost too curious for his own good. One day this monkey was sitting in a tree by the water when a great fish came swimming by and offered him a ride.

The curious monkey climbed onto the fish's back. But when they were far out at sea, the fish said, "I meant to tell you that I am taking you to my king, who is very sick and can only be cured by eating the heart of a monkey."

Quickly the monkey said to the fish, "You should have told me about your king before we started. I left my heart hanging back in the tree. We shall have to go back for it."

The stupid fish turned around and brought the monkey back to the shore, where he scrambled to safety at the top of his tree.

THE DOG

Since the most ancient times, the dog has been a part of African village life throughout the continent. Many fables tell how it happened that the dog instead of the jackal or hyena came to live with man. But African dogs were not pets. They were treated like any other useful animal, and they were expected to earn their keep by hunting, catching rats, and serving as watchdogs.

In the Congo, the dog often appears in carvings that were used for magic. A divining board, the Itombwa, often had a head shaped like a dog, or a crocodile, or a human being. On the flattened back of the Itombwa was a small knob, which the medicine man moved back and forth as he asked questions. When the knob stuck, it was a sign that the answer was Yes.

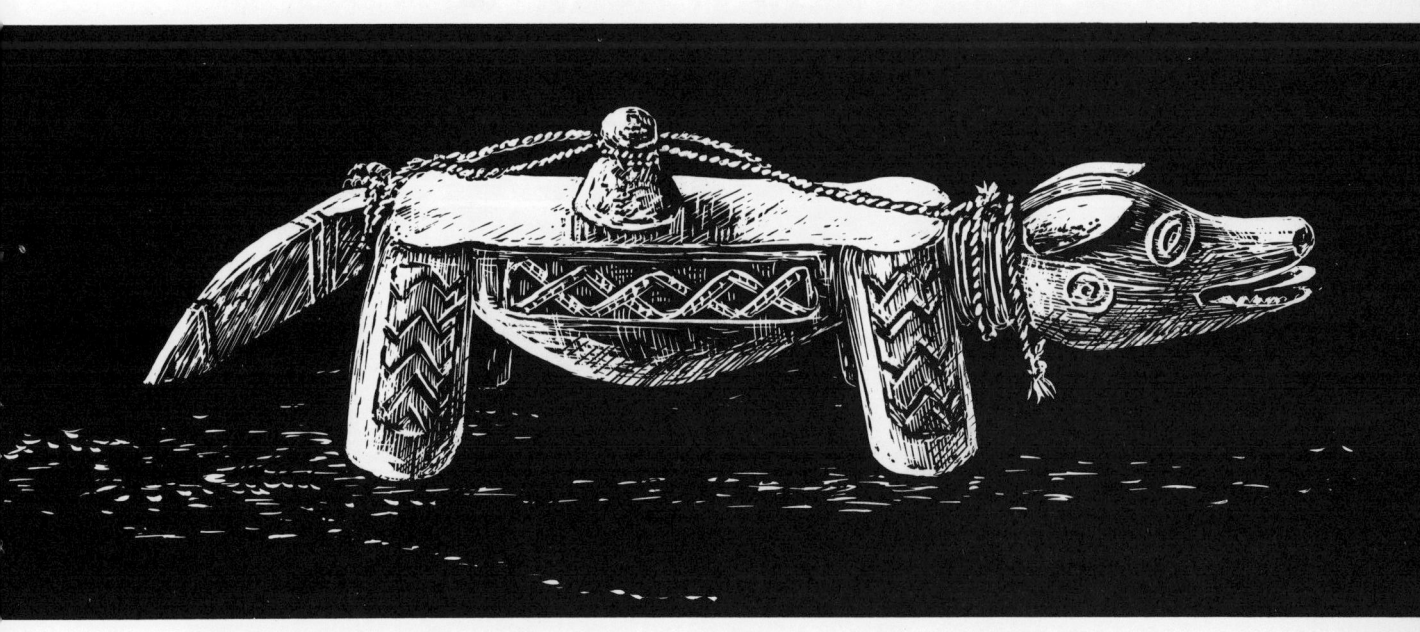

Spirits were believed to have helped move the knob on the flat back of this carved wooden Itombwa.

Another carving used for magic was the Konde, which had the shape of a dog (or other figure). It was made from a log of up to six feet long, and it was supposed to be inhabited by a powerful spirit. To awaken this spirit and get his attention, a nail was driven into the Konde. The spirit would respond by witnessing an agreement or granting a favor. The Konde was also used to test guilt. If an accused man was guilty, he became ill when the nail was driven into the Konde. In the hands of a wise medicine man, this magic was helpful in enforcing order. In the wrong hands, the Konde could be turned to evil use.

This Konde had only a few nails pounded into the wooden shape. Nails were often just slabs of iron. But over many years of use, such a figure could become completely studded with iron pieces and nails. The medicine man of the Bakongo tribe inserted magical substances, such as pieces of teeth and sticky gums, into the hole in the back of the Konde. A disturbed or angry person was helped by the effort needed to drive the iron nail into the wood and by his belief in the power of the fearful spirit inside.

A water spirit headdress.

Reptiles and Fish

Of sea gods and totems

Throughout Africa, waterways once provided an important means of transportation. Dugout canoes or reed boats carried men easily where thick forest or rocks and cliffs made land travel difficult.

But although Africans often traveled on the water, very few of them swam in it, because of the crocodile. This powerful and dangerous creature can easily kill a man. Only a few centuries ago, the crocodile was plentiful in almost every waterway in Africa.

THE CROCODILE

In both magic and religion, the crocodile received much attention. For example, the Ashanti and certain other tribes revered the crocodile as a totem. They believed that the totem creature was the founder of their tribe, or that it had saved the

The little double crocodile illustrated an Ashanti fable. The two foolish crocodile heads fought over which should get some food, even though they had but one stomach. The moral of the fable applied to family life: Think about the good of the whole group, not just oneself.

life of one of their important ancestors. Thus, the totem animal was related to every member of a family or of the tribe, and it was forbidden to harm or eat it. A great variety of creatures are totems to various families and, like the crocodile, all totem animals are both feared and respected.

Among the Basuto, it was believed that a crocodile could grab a man's shadow and pull him into the water. In other tribes, it was thought that if a man killed a crocodile, he would turn into one. When a crocodile attacked a man, it was thought that it might be a dead man in crocodile form, who had come to avenge some wrong.

From the Bakongo tribe comes this fable. At the water's edge, a hen was about to be eaten by a crocodile. Quickly she called out, "Brother, do not eat your kin!" She was spared. Thereafter, the same thing happened every time the hen came down to the water to drink. But the crocodile was puzzled about the hen's remark. Finally, he went to the wise turtle and asked, "How can a crocodile be brother to a hen?"

"Foolish crocodile," replied the turtle, "do you not come from an egg? The hen comes from an egg, and so do the other birds and the lizard, as well as I myself. We are all brothers."

A crocodile with a snake was part of a design carved on a wooden door by the Senufo people.

This ivory gong, carved by the craftsmen of Benin, sounded two notes. The sound was said to be the laughter of the king. As the king of Benin was so above his people, he was not allowed to show any emotions such as laughter. Therefore, when he wished to laugh, he would hit the gong with an ivory mallet. Designs showing the king, his courtiers and sometimes his musicians were carved in the ivory. Surrounding these figures were various, other creatures such as turtles, birds, bats and snakes. On the side of the gong shown, the Oba (king) appeared as a sea god with mudfish legs.

THE MUDFISH AND THE CHAMELEON

In Nigeria, the god of water and wealth was Olokun, and the sacred fish was the mudfish. These fish appeared often on the beautiful decorative plaques of Benin, a city-kingdom which ruled part of what is now Nigeria. To show the king's connection with Olokun, the king of Benin was sometimes portrayed with two mudfish where his legs should have been.

A chameleon carved of wood and painted with bright designs by the Bobo tribe.

Olokun also appears in one myth about the chameleon, the little lizard which has the ability to change its color to match its surroundings. Once, the sky and the sea were arguing as to which was wealthiest and should therefore rule supreme. The sky god sent the chameleon as a messenger to Olokun, to escort him to a meeting.

When Olokun came out of his water palace, he saw that the chameleon was as richly dressed as he. The god became annoyed and went back to put on more lavish robes, more gold and coral ornaments. But again he found the messenger just as richly dressed. Seven times the sea god tried to outdo the lowly messenger and failed. Then Olokun had to admit that the sky god must indeed be the richest if he could dress even his servant so gorgeously. That is how the sky became supreme.

This decorative bronze fish was a tiny Ashanti gold weight.

THE LIZARD In some areas of Africa the lizard, chameleon, snake, and other small creatures were known as "bush souls," for it was believed that such animals could share a certain part of a man's soul. The man and his bush soul were thought to be linked together. If the animal which shared part of his soul were injured, the man would feel pain in the same part of his body. This belief gave people a reason for having certain aches and sicknesses which could not otherwise be explained. The idea of bush soul is also a vivid example of the oneness of the human and animal worlds in African thought.

To some tribes, lizards were believed to be souls of the dead; other tribes believed them to be bush souls or totems. In ancient Chad, a legend says, a great building was being constructed. To ensure that it would never fall, a sacrifice had to be made. Three young princesses were walled up inside and left to die. Their spirits became lizards. Thereafter, the custom was to take each newly chosen leader to a hole in a certain wall of that building. If lizards (which often live in cracks in masonry) appeared, then the spirits approved of the new leader.

THE SNAKE From the beginning of time, people have believed that snakes have special powers. Since the snake can shed its skin and still live, it has been regarded as a symbol of the endless circle of life, death, and rebirth. It is often shown with its tail in its mouth, so that it forms a circle.

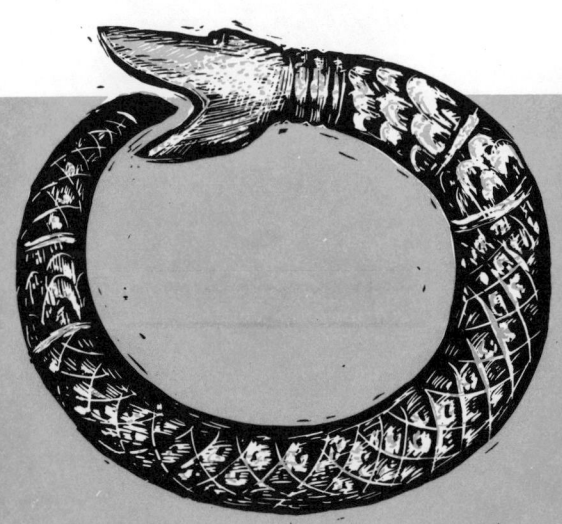

To the people of Dahomey, the snake was very important in their religion, charms, magic and stories. This snake was shown with his tail in his mouth to make the endless circle of life, death and rebirth.

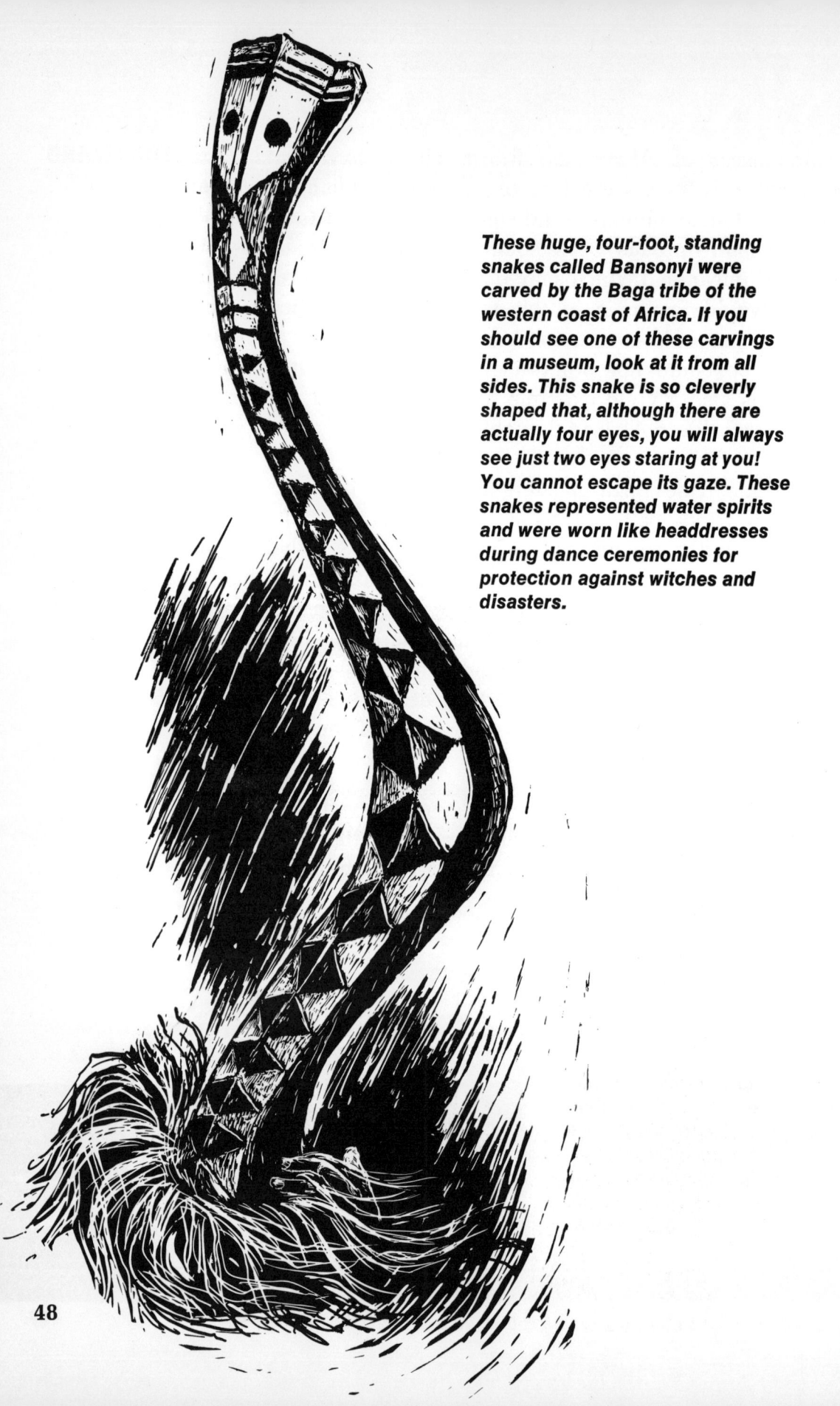

These huge, four-foot, standing snakes called Bansonyi were carved by the Baga tribe of the western coast of Africa. If you should see one of these carvings in a museum, look at it from all sides. This snake is so cleverly shaped that, although there are actually four eyes, you will always see just two eyes staring at you! You cannot escape its gaze. These snakes represented water spirits and were worn like headdresses during dance ceremonies for protection against witches and disasters.

Because of its shape, the snake seemed to have other special meanings for Africans. Its slithering was related to basic motions such as running water or curling smoke. A snake also suggested other things that are important to life, such as the roots of a tree or the umbilical cord that links a newborn child to its mother. In many areas of ancient Africa, these ideas were portrayed in jewelry and carvings.

In several parts of the land, the snake, or sometimes a pair of snakes, was connected to the appearance of an arching rainbow. In Dahomey and some areas of ancient Nigeria, this snake-shaped rainbow was a very favorable sign. It meant that the land would bear good crops and the people would have many children.

From the Niger River area comes the myth of Mawu, the creator god, who was carried over the world on the back of the great snake, Aido Hwedo. Wherever they rested at night, great mountains formed. But the mountains soon became too heavy for the earth. Mawu asked Aido Hwedo to curl himself beneath the mountains to support them.

The great snake obeyed, but he found it very hot work. Then Mawu made the oceans and poured them around the snake to keep him cool. Aido Hwedo has been there ever since, this legend says, holding up the land. If he ever gets hungry, he may have to eat his tail, and then the world will fall down. Whenever he shifts his position a bit, there is an earthquake.

This snake, part of a picture sewn on fabric, represented the rainbow snake.

The myth of the snake which holds up the world appears in many forms. Some say that the posts which hold up the corners of the land are supported by snakes. Others tell how the snake's coils move around and around, creating the motion of the earth and stars. In all stories, one finds the belief that the world is a living moving thing.

Legends about snakes may also be based on history, as is shown in the following example from ancient Ghana. This prosperous kingdom was protected from misfortune by Ouagadou-Bida, the sacred serpent. But to save his sweetheart, a young man named Amadou fought with the serpent and killed it. With each blow Amadou struck, pieces of the serpent flew great distances into the air. Wherever they fell to earth, gold fields were formed. Then, as was predicted, disaster followed the death of the sacred serpent. Drought and famine ended the days of greatness of the kingdom.

Large bronze python head, probably part of a snake decoration that once guarded a gateway into the Benin palace.

These flying birds, carved by the Senufo, were carried on poles. Sometimes a pole of this kind was a prize to the young man who best prepared the ground for planting of crops. It was awarded at spring ceremonies.

wild birds

And other winged things

There are thousands of species of birds in Africa, from the great ostrich of the grasslands to the tiny birds that dwell in the forest. It is not surprising, therefore, that birds are a part of African folklore and myth and that they appear in many ornaments and pieces of sculpture.

Some African carved birds are easy to identify as real, whereas others are imaginary. For example, a bird was sometimes made with wings in the shape of a spiral, which is unlike those of any real bird. To some Africans the spiral (as seen also in the snail and seashell) represented growth, increasing steadily from the center. Thus, the bird with spiral wings was a symbol of growth for their crops and families.

Birds of various kinds often appeared in Ashanti gold weights.

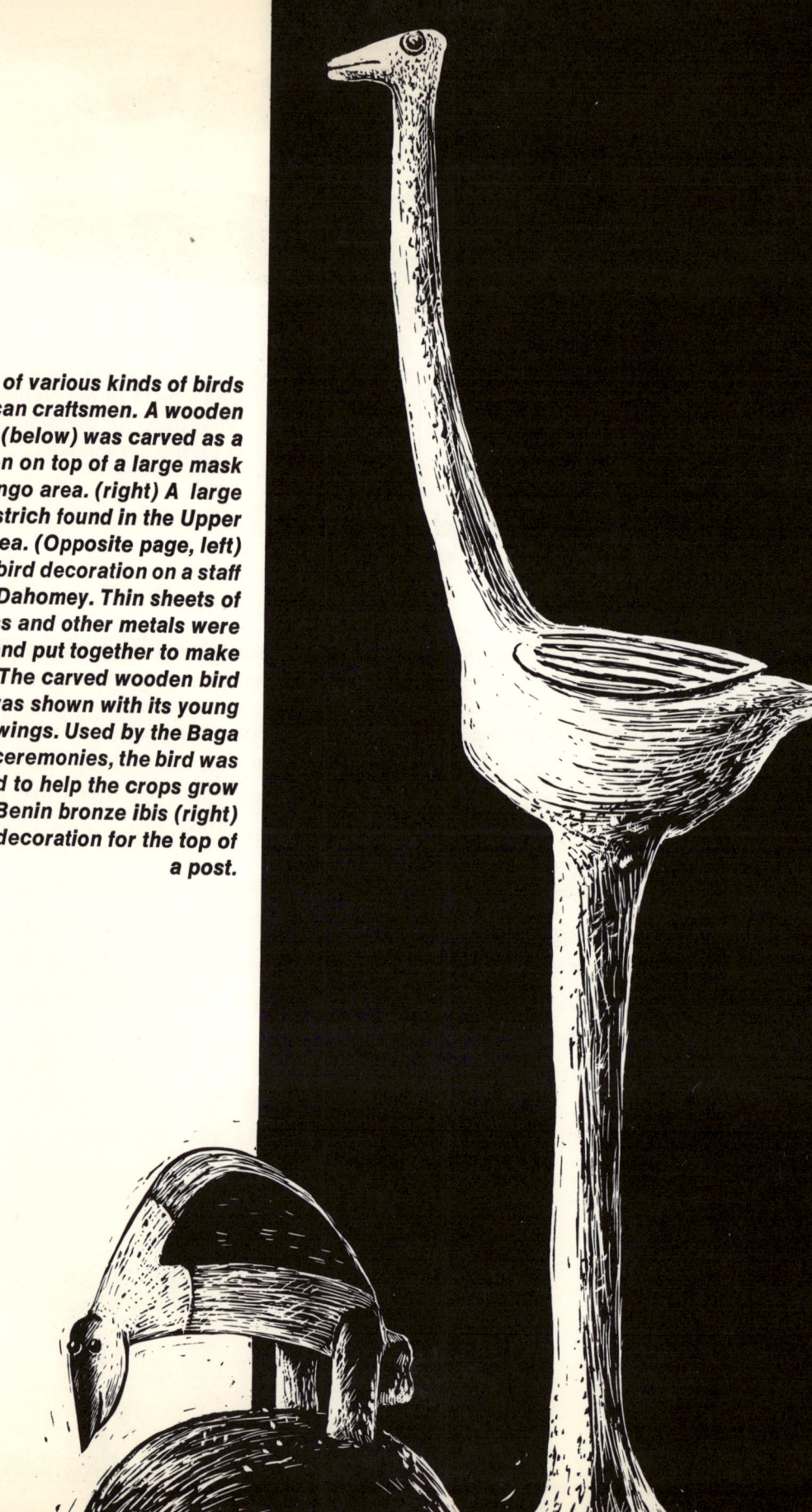

A group of various kinds of birds from African craftsmen. A wooden bird (below) was carved as a decoration on top of a large mask in the Congo area. (right) A large bronze ostrich found in the Upper Niger area. (Opposite page, left) A large bird decoration on a staff from Dahomey. Thin sheets of brass and other metals were shaped and put together to make this bird. The carved wooden bird (center) was shown with its young on its wings. Used by the Baga tribe in ceremonies, the bird was believed to help the crops grow well. The Benin bronze ibis (right) was a decoration for the top of a post.

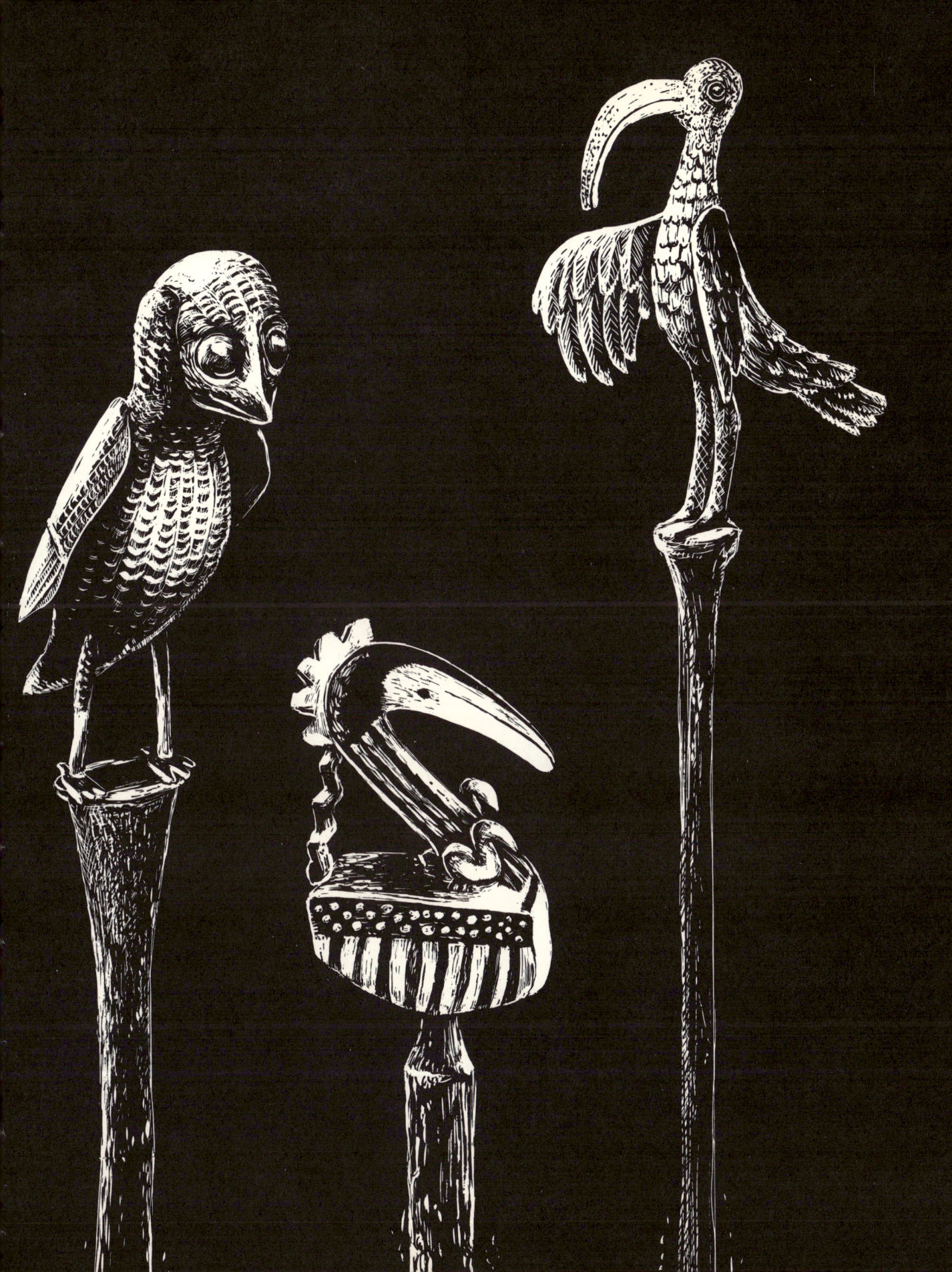

Another meaning was given to the bird form in the court of ancient Mali. There, once a year, a man in a bird's-head mask and feathered costume was allowed to come before the king and say whatever he wished without fear of punishment. On that one day, the bird-messenger told the king what his people really thought of him and made sure their complaints were heard.

Some Yoruba tribes also saw the bird as a messenger. Among these tribes, the messages the bird brought were supposed to come from the dead. Some of the Yoruba medicine men were skilled in ventriloquism, which is the art of throwing the voice so that it seems to come from some other source than the speaker. The medicine men could thus carry on "conversations" with the tribe's ancestors, whose voices might seem to come from the figure of an iron bird on a staff.

This pair of metal birds, possibly hornbills, were made in the Ivory Coast area.

THE HORNBILL

This rather heavy-bodied bird has a large bill and a most unusual nesting habit. After the eggs have been laid in a hole in a tree, the female hornbill shuts herself inside the hole by building a stout wall of mud and other material. During the time when the eggs are hatching and later when the young birds are defenseless, the male feeds them through a small hole in the mud wall. In this way, the hornbill keeps his family safe from monkeys, snakes, and other enemies.

In view of these habits, it is not surprising that the hornbill often appears in African folklore as an example of family love. The female not only shuts herself up to make her children safe, but she also keeps the nest clean by throwing debris and droppings out through the feeding hole.

The hornbill was a favorite subject of Ashanti craftsmen. The one on the left was carved of wood, the other was a small bronze sculpture for the palace.

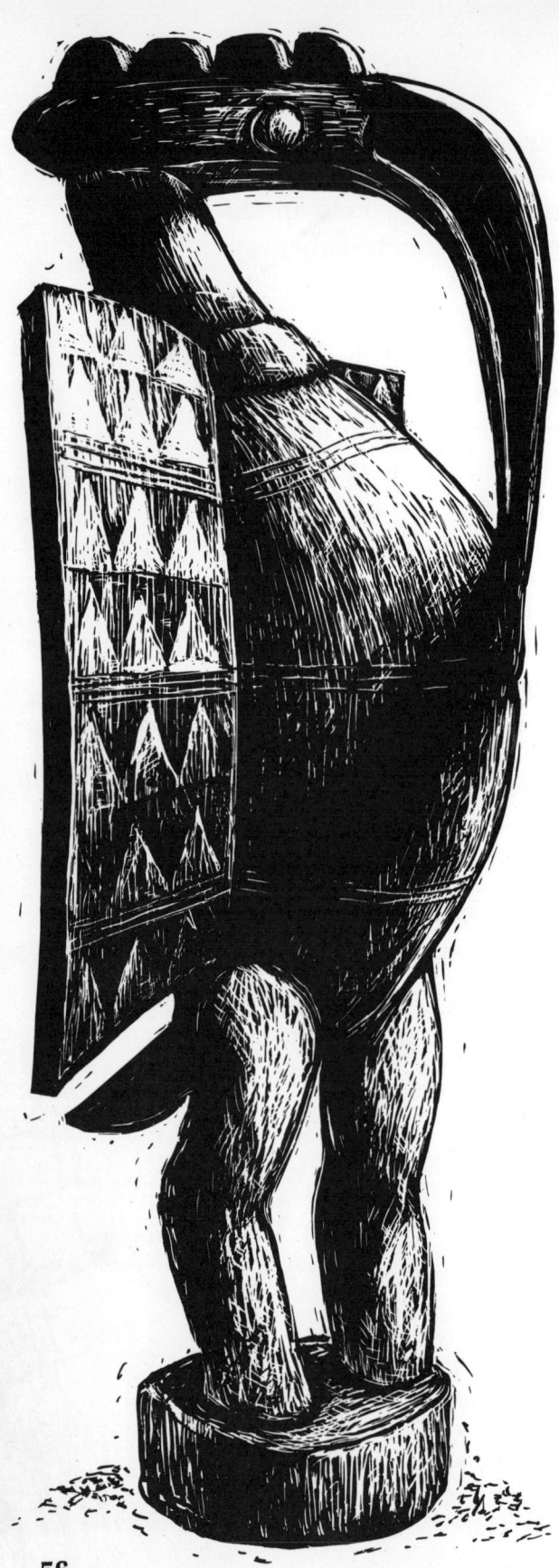

To the Senufo people, the hornbill also had a religious meaning. It was supposed to have been one of the first five creatures on earth and to have provided the first food for man. Statues of the hornbill (sometimes as large as four feet high) show the bird as protector of the tribe. Sometimes, small birds are carved on the statue's wings. They are a reminder that the hornbill guards its own young from harm, and they show the tribe's hope that its people will have many children.

Huge standing statue of the hornbill called Porpianong. It meant the continuation of life for the Senufo. Although the wooden carvings were heavy, it is believed they were carried or held on the head during ceremonies. The Porpianong showed the hornbill in many ways, but always standing, with a large beak and belly. Often they were painted with red and white triangles.

THE EAGLE AND THE HAWK

It is a common African belief that lightning is a great and powerful bird, like the eagle or the hawk. Some of the Bantu tribes of central Africa put up posts with these birds carved on the top, in the hope that lightning will strike the posts and not the houses.

The walls around the ancient stone fortress of Zimbabwe had posts with similar hawklike birds on them. Were they also meant to draw the lightning? No one knows. Some think the birds had nothing to do with lightning, but possibly were meant to bring messages to the king from the dead. Whatever they meant, the impressive statues of Zimbabwe were the work of highly skilled artists.

Stone Zimbabwe carving shows a crocodile-like creature crawling up a post that is topped by a strange, powerful bird.

THE BAT In some parts of Africa, witches were believed to be evil spirits that were able to take control of the body of a person or animal at night. Since bats fly in the dark, they were often thought to be creatures which were inhabited by witch-spirits, just as a man's body might at times be inhabited by a witch-spirit. A person's nightmares were believed to result from a spirit that occupied his body during the night.

The night-flying habits of the bat were also the basis for the fable about the bat's feud with the sun. It seems that long ago the bat flew in the daytime. Then the bat's mother became very ill. The antelope told the bat that only the sun could cure his mother. But the sun told the bat that it was too busy to visit the bat's mother. In the end, the bat's mother died.

The bat asked all the other animals to come to his mother's funeral, but they refused. They said the bat was no relation to them because he could fly like a bird. Then the bat asked all the birds to the funeral, but they too refused. They said the bat could not be a bird because he had no feathers. The bat buried his mother alone and, ever since, he has refused to come out in daytime.

Large wooden mask carved by the Bambara is believed to have been a bat with horns of an antelope. What spirit it was meant to represent is unknown.

The butterfly was a sign of spring to the Bobo. These decorative masks representing birds and butterflies were part of dances at planting time. During the ceremony, masks were twirled about by the dancers.

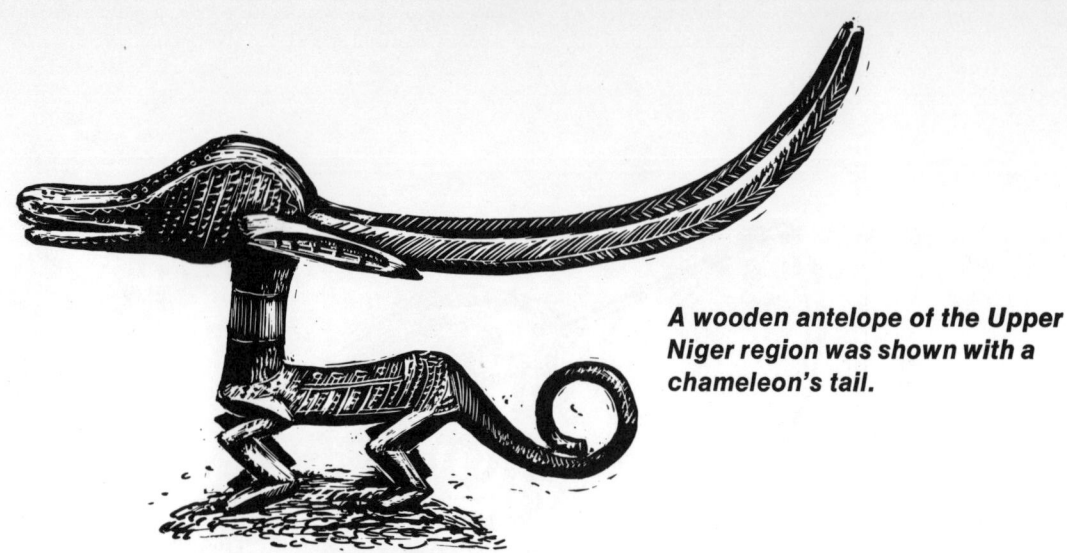

A wooden antelope of the Upper Niger region was shown with a chameleon's tail.

conclusion

Today, Africa is changing fast. Many of its animal species are threatened by human beings, who want to hunt them or to build and farm on land which was once wild. The tribal way of life is also disappearing. With it go the arts and crafts, as well as the understanding of animals, which produced the sculpted, carved, and painted creatures that appear in this book.

We have seen that animals in African art showed not only the artist's talent and training, but also something about the way different African peoples felt about the animals around them. Because each artist put some of his own feelings into his work, each piece of art is different from the others.

The best way to appreciate African art is by looking at it in person instead of looking at pictures. Some museums have permanent African collections, such as the Museum of Natural History in New York City. Most museums have at least a few pieces. Check your local museum, or watch for special exhibitions.

suggested further reading

If you want to read more African folklore, here is a list of interesting books:

Aardema, Verna. **The Sky-God Stories.** New York: Coward-McCann, Inc. 1960. (and other books by this author)

Arnott, Kathleen. **Tales of Temba.** New York: Henry Z. Walck, Inc., 1969.

Burton, W. **The Magic Drum.** New York: Criterion Books, 1962.

Courlander, Harold. **The Hat-Shaking Dance, and Other Tales from the Gold Coast.** New York: Harcourt, Brace & World, 1957. (and other books by this author)

Guillot, René. **Guillot's African Folk Tales.** New York: Franklin Watts, Inc., 1964.

Harman, Humphrey. **Tales Told Near A Crocodile.** New York: The Viking Press, Inc., 1967.

Heady, Eleanor. **When the Stones Were Soft.** New York: Funk & Wagnalls, 1968.

Kuala, Edna Mason. **African Village Folktales.** New York: World Publishing Company, 1968.

Savory, Phyllis. **Congo Fireside Tales.** New York: Hastings House, Publishers, Inc., 1962.

Sturton, Hugh. **Zomo, the Rabbit.** New York: Atheneum Publishers, 1966.

Tracey, Hugh. **The Lion on the Path.** New York: Praeger Publishers, Inc., 1967.

Walker, Barbara K. **The Dancing Palm Tree.** New York: Parents' Magazine Press, 1968.

Woodson, Carter Godwin. **African Myths, Together with Proverbs.** Associated Publishing, 1964.

Historical Maps

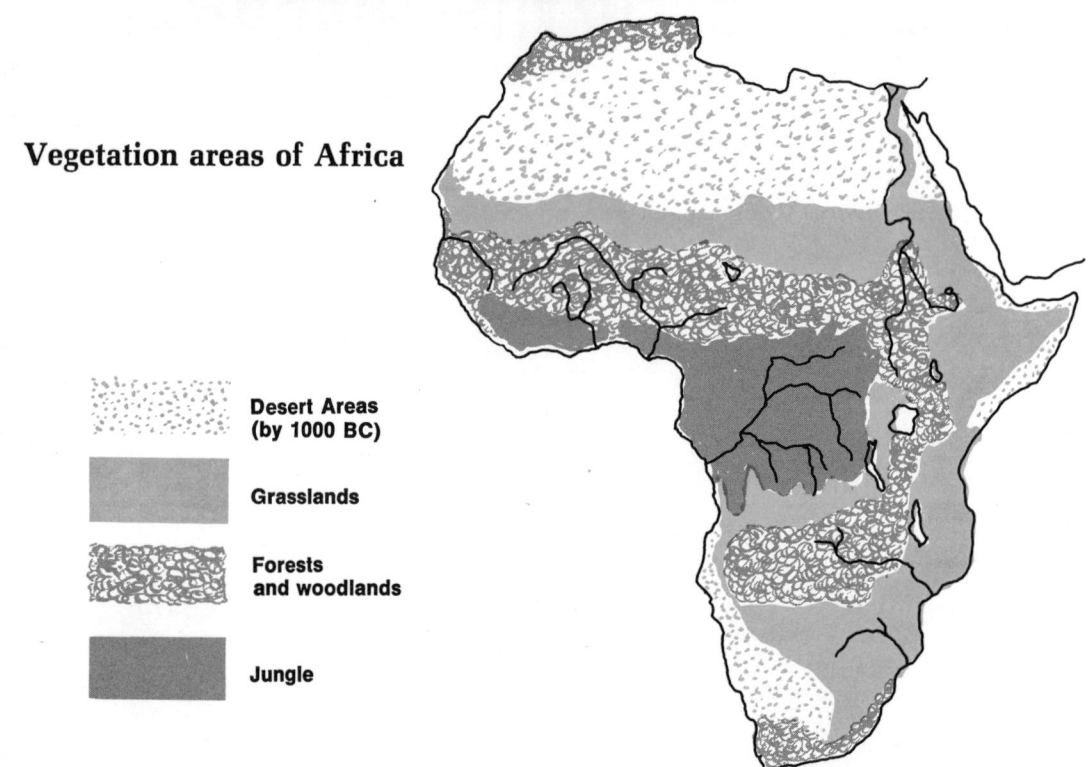

Vegetation areas of Africa

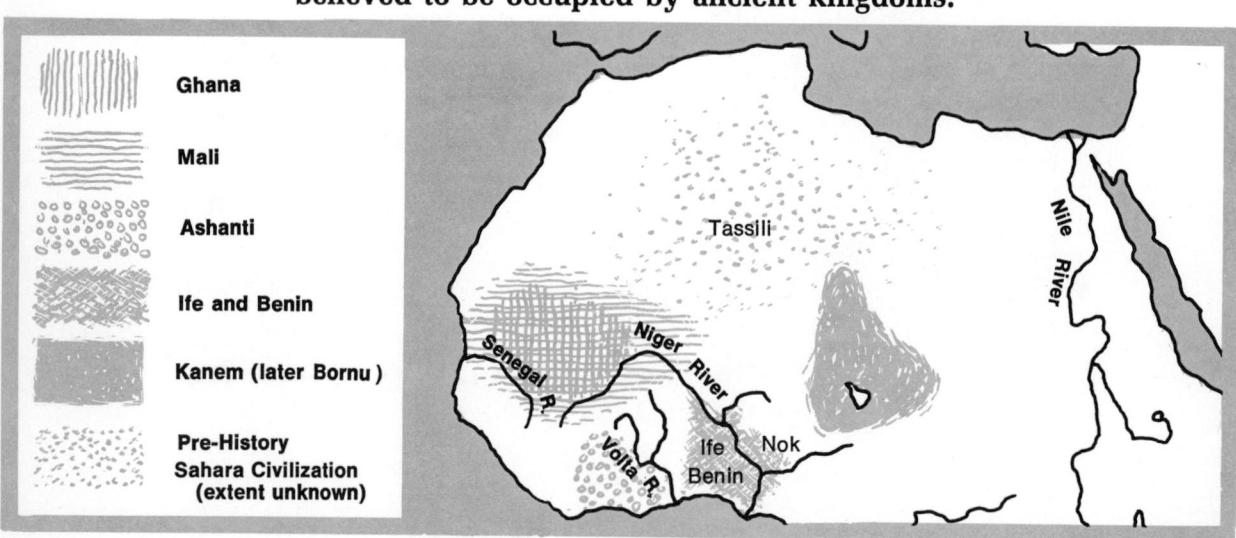

Detail of western Africa showing general areas believed to be occupied by ancient kingdoms.

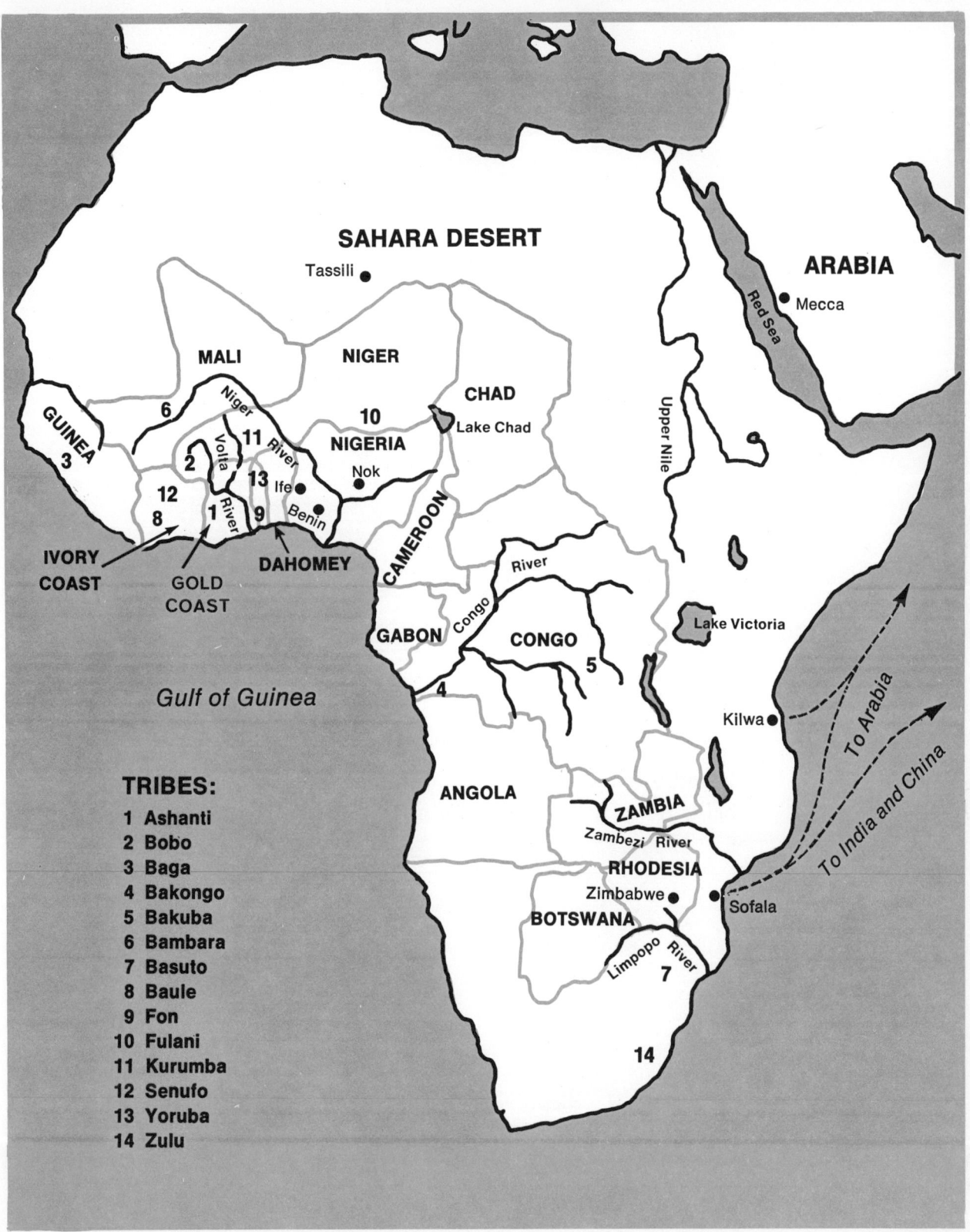